Migrant Worker

A Boy from the Rio Grande Valley

Library of Congress Cataloging-in-Publication Data
Hoyt-Goldsmith, Diane
    Migrant worker: a boy from the Rio Grande Valley / by Diane Hoyt-Goldsmith:
photographs by Lawrence Migdale.
        p.   cm.
Includes index.
    Summary: Describes the way of life of Mexican-American families
and their children who work as migrant agricultural laborers in Texas.
    ISBN 0-8234-1225-3 (hardcover : alk. paper)
    1. Mexican American agricultural laborers — Texas — Lower Rio Grande Valley — Juvenile literature. 2. Migrant agricultural
laborers — Texas — Lower Rio Grande Valley — Juvenile literature. 3. Mexican American families — Texas — Lower Rio Grande
Valley — Juvenile Literature. 4. Mexican American children — Employment — Texas — Lower Rio Grande Valley — Juvenile
Literature. [1. Mexican Americans — Texas. 2. Migrant labor. 3. Agricultural laborers.] I. Migdale, Lawrence, ill. II. Title.
HD1527.T4H69 1996
331.5'44'097644--dc20

Acknowledgments
    We would like to thank the Benitez family — Olga and Martin and the children: Martin, Adriana, Enrique, Ricardo, and Edith —
for their hospitality and cooperation. They made us feel very welcome in Rio Grande City.
    We give special thanks to Encarnacion "Chon" Garza and his family: Alda, Alissa, and Alejandra. Chon shared the joy that he
experienced as he observed his students "reaching for the stars" and achieving their goals.
    Thanks to Lupe Amador, Jr., Elias Saenz, Alda Garza, and the entire staff and student body of Ringgold Elementary School. In
spite of being located in one of the poorest counties in the United States, the school has a rich atmosphere. It fosters enthusiasm
for learning and pride in one's culture.
    We would also like to acknowledge some very special young people who took the time to share their experiences with us:
Beatriz (Betty) Lopez, Edith Benitez, Orlando Sandoval, Luisana Barrera, and Laura Barrera. They were candid and direct, and we
greatly appreciate their contributions. Oscar Vasquez, the manager of Ringgold Farms, was kind enough to allow us to spend time
in the fields, to take photographs, and to observe the harvest. We thank him for that opportunity.
    Thanks to Gloria Hernandez, on the staff of CRLA, for her reading of the manuscript and suggestions. Ms.
Hernandez was also a migrant child in the Rio Grande Valley and traveled to work in the fields of San Joaquin Valley
in California.
    We appreciate the suggestions of Margery Cuyler, our editor, and Lorna Mason, who gave us historical perspective.
    And thanks to Abe Bonowitz of the César E. Chávez Foundation, P.O. Box 62, Keene, CA 93531, for reviewing the manuscript
and for his helpful comments. For more information about the life of César E. Chávez, please contact César E. Chávez Foundation,
P.O. Box 62, Keene, CA 93531. 805-822-5571, Ext. 256, or E-mail <Chavezfdtn @ 19c.apc.org).

Migrant Worker
A Boy from the Rio Grande Valley

by Diane Hoyt-Goldsmith
photographs by Lawrence Migdale

Holiday House · New York

This book is dedicated to the memory of

César Chávez,

(1927 – 1993),

a man who dedicated his life

to improving the working conditions

of migrants in the United States.

My name is Ricardo, but all my friends call me Ricky.
I am eleven years old and in the fifth grade at Ringgold
Elementary School in Rio Grande City, Texas. The place
where I live is close to the Rio Grande, the river that
flows between Texas and Mexico. It gives our town its
name and is only a few miles from my house.

The Rio Grande marks the border between the United States and Mexico. We call the area just north of the river *la frontera (lah fron-TEHR-rah)*, which means "the border" in Spanish. Like my family, many people living in Texas towns along the Rio Grande have moved to the United States from Mexico.

At home, most of us speak Spanish. Our way of life and culture is the same as it is for those who live across the river in Mexico. My parents came to the United States because there are better jobs here, but they are proud of their Mexican heritage.

I was born in Miguel Alemán *(mee-GEL ah-lay-MON)*, a small town in Mexico. I am the youngest of five children. I have two older brothers and two older sisters. Their names are Martin *(mar-TEEN)*, Adriana *(ah-dree-ANH-nah)*, Enrique *(en-REE-kay)*, and Edith.

(Top) Ricky's mother lights candles every day on the small altar next to the refrigerator in the kitchen. Like most Mexican-Americans, she and her family are Catholic.

(Right) Ricky's mother makes Mexican food for her family. They like to eat tacos with refried beans and arroz mexicano (ah-ROHS meh-hee-KAH-noh), *Mexican rice.*

Ricky helps his mother with chores in the yard. Each member of the family has a few small jobs. In this way, everyone shares in running the house.

During the school year, my mother stays at home and takes care of us. My father works hundreds of miles away in Chicago where he has found a very good job. He operates large machines for a company that is building roads. He sends most of his wages home to support the six of us in Texas.

Because traveling back and forth is so expensive, he can only come home to visit on special occasions. Sometimes I don't see him for months at a time. I really miss him. When he does visit, he plays catch with me, and we spend a lot of time together.

Ricky's father comes home to celebrate Adriana's quinceañera (KEEN-say-ahn-NEYR-rah). This is a special party given by parents when their daughter reaches the age of fifteen. The family invites fifteen boys and fifteen girls to be "damas" and "chamberlains." They join many other guests at a fancy party and dance. The quinceañera is an important custom for the Mexican people.

7

My Neighborhood

There isn't enough space in Ricky's house for him to have a room of his own. He has to sleep on a couch in the living room. Before turning out the light, he reads a chapter in his biology book to prepare for a test at school.

The Mexican-American neighborhoods along the border are called *colonias (coh-LONE-ee-ahs)*. These are large developments in which people can buy a building lot and construct a house. Owning a home is an important goal for Mexican immigrants.

New families from Mexico usually cannot afford to hire a construction company. Most people find members of their family or friends with enough skills to help them build a house.

Sometimes people trade goods for services. One friend might know how to install plumbing. Another might be able to get a good price on windows. Often it takes people years to finish building a house, but by working with others, they are able to do it.

The houses vary in size, in style, and in the way they are built. Some are large and fancy, with brick walls and lots of bedrooms. Others in the same block are no more than one-room shacks.

In several colonias, the developers have not planned well for services such as water, sewers, and electricity. In a few cases, people run an extension cord from one house to another to bring in electricity. Sometimes the only running water comes from a garden hose. Roads in the colonias, if they exist at all, are often bumpy, rough, and poorly constructed.

Each colonia has a special name. The one we live in is called the Garza Salinas Subdivision. Garza *(GAR-zah)* is the Spanish name for a white heron and Salinas *(sah-LEE-nahs)* means "a place to make salt." Some other colonias nearby are called Arroyo *(ah-ROY-yoh)*, which means "a riverbed," and Las Lomas *(las LOH-mahs)*, which means "the hills."

(Top) The foundation of cement blocks in this colonia is the beginning of a new home. As soon as people buy land in the colonia, they start building. When they run out of money, the construction stops. Sometimes a partly built house will remain that way for months or even years.

(Right) Ricky and his sister, Edith, play a board game while listening to a baseball game on television. In Rio Grande City, the kids like rock- and-roll music, but their favorite radio stations play tejano (teh-HAHN-noh) music. These songs, sung in Spanish, are accompanied by accordions and guitars and have a beat that's good for dancing.

9

The Rio Grande Valley

The part of Texas where I live has rich soil and many large farms. Driving down the highway between Rio Grande City and McAllen, the nearest big city, crops on both sides of the road stretch to the horizon. The landscape is flat, the weather is warm, and there is lots of rain.

We have the perfect climate for growing all kinds of fruits and vegetables. Farms grow cantaloupes, honeydew melons, bell peppers, onions, cabbages, and watermelons. There are also large fields planted with sorghum (*SAWR*-guhm), a crop that provides feed for cattle and other animals.

Because Rio Grande City is located near the border, many businesses in Ricky's town have signs in both English and Spanish. Raspas (RAHS-pahs) is Spanish for "snow cones."

10

(Top) Sorghum is one of the most important crops grown in the Rio Grande Valley.

(Right) Ricky enjoys eating sandia (san-DEE-ah), *the Spanish word for "watermelon," another valuable crop that grows in the fields near his home.*

My Job

Although I am only eleven years old, I am a migrant worker. During the summers, I travel with my family to distant farms to work in the fields with other migrant children and their families. We find jobs on large farms that need a work force that can expand or shrink, depending on the season of the year.

For example, during the winter when the fields are empty, just a few people on huge tractors are needed to prepare the land for planting. Once the seeds have started to grow, however, many people are hired to hoe or pull the weeds in the fields. This is a job that must be done by people instead of machines. A machine cannot tell a weed from a cotton seedling, but a person can.

Later in the summer, when the crops ripen, lots of workers are needed to pick fruits and vegetables over a short period of time. Then large numbers of workers pack the harvest for market. After the crop has been picked and packed, those workers will no longer have jobs. They will move farther north to pick the crops that have ripened on the farms there.

Most migrant workers are given the jobs that must be done by hand. This kind of work is called manual labor and it does not require a lot of education. Migrant workers need to have strong bodies and a willingness to work outside in all kinds of weather.

Migrants work long hours. Often we are in the fields for ten, eleven, or twelve hours a day. Most jobs do not pay well. On some farms, people are not even paid a minimum wage.

Teams of workers harvest a melon crop. As a tractor moves slowly through the fields, workers place ripened melons on a conveyor belt that takes them up to a trailer behind the tractor. When the trailer is full, it is disconnected and hauled by truck to a packing shed.

For this reason, all the members of migrant families work together. Each family member helps out, even the young children. The smallest children carry empty picking baskets to their parents, or bring them water to drink.

Unlike most migrant families, we try to stay in one place during the school year. Then in June, when school is out, we hit the road and travel north to help with the cotton crop. I went to work in the fields for the first time last summer, when I was ten years old.

(Top) Migrant workers in the Rio Grande Valley of Texas.

MIGRANT PATTERNS FOR FARM WORKERS IN THE UNITED STATES

Pacific Coast – Workers pick vegetables and fruits.

Texas – Migrants work on sugar beet, cotton, and vegetable farms.

Atlantic Coast – Workers pick produce and work in the cotton fields.

US Department of Labor, Bureau of Labor Standards

(Left) This map shows the migration patterns for workers in the United States. There are three large areas in the country where migrants have their home base. Most spend the winters in California, Florida, or Texas. These states have a long growing season and there is always some work to be done in the fields, even in the cooler months. Then, in the summer, as the crops ripen in the northern states, laborers migrate there to work on the farms.

Ricky picks only the melons that are ripe. He has been taught to tell if they are ripe by judging their color, size, and the way they feel. Ricky puts the melons into a shoulder bag. When the bag is full, it is very heavy. Ricky carries the bag to a large trailer where the melons are unloaded.

A Day in the Fields

What is it like to work in the fields? I can tell you. We have to wake up at five o'clock every morning when it is still dark. My mother makes breakfast and then packs a lunch for us to take and eat later in the day.

We dress in layers because the mornings are cool. By the end of the day, however, we are down to only a shirt and pants. It gets very hot and we sweat a lot. We wear old clothes because we get dirty when we work.

Sometimes the plants in the fields have been sprayed with chemicals that kill weeds or insects. My mother worries because these poisons can rub off on us. To protect ourselves, we always wear long sleeves, even when it's hot.

I wear a hat and a bandanna to keep the sun from burning my neck as I bend over to work. Some of the men don't wear hats because they want to be *macho* (MAH-cho) or manly. I would rather be comfortable.

My family rides to the fields in our truck. We arrive just as the sun is coming up. My mom and dad, my brothers, my sisters, and I all work together. After about five hours, we take time off to rest. Our arms and legs and backs hurt from bending over. I feel so hungry and tired, all I want to do is lie down in a cool place and eat. I enjoy the tacos and fruit that my mother has fixed for us. I drink some soda and relax. Just when I'm starting to feel good, it's time to go back to work again.

The best part about traveling to work during the summer is that my whole family is together. My father comes home from Chicago to join us. I'm glad to be with my father again, even if we can't talk much or have fun when we are in the fields. We try to make up for it on our day off.

A worker dumps Ricky's bag of melons into a trailer. Ricky will take the empty bag back to the row where he was working and fill it up again.

Every few hours, the workers get a rest break for thirty minutes. Usually there is water available for the migrants when they get thirsty. On some farms like this one, the farmer provides portable outhouses for the workers. Unfortunately, this isn't true of every farm.

15

Ricky and Edith shop for groceries on their day off.

Cars and pedestrians cross the bridge between Roma in Texas and Miguel Alemán in Mexico.

My family gets paid every Sunday. The boss gives one check to my parents for the whole family. Then we go cash it. All of the money goes to support our family, but sometimes my parents give us a little spending money for a treat, a movie, or for something we need. My mother and father try to save as much as they can.

While we are working away from home, we have to pay our own expenses. We buy the food that we eat and pay the rent on our temporary housing. Usually, we stay in a motel or rent a small apartment in the town near the farm where we work. We have to pay the bills for electricity and water, too.

Sometimes we stay in a labor camp. That is a place with lots of tiny houses where migrant workers live. Often the camps are located in small farming communities. The really large farms have their own labor camps.

My mother does not like us to stay in the labor camps if something else is available, since the houses are not always clean. They are tiny, and there isn't much room for a big family like ours.

Sunday is our only holiday from work. At home in Rio Grande City, we go to church. But when we are traveling, we spend our day off at a shopping mall. It has air-conditioning, which feels nice after working in the hot sun all week. We like to walk around and look in the store windows. Sometimes we go to see a movie or play video games in an arcade. It's fun.

I don't like to work in the fields all day because it is *muy duro (mooey DUR-oh)*. In Spanish that means that it is "very hard." But I know it is important to help my family, so I try to do it without complaining. Working in the fields makes me appreciate how hard my parents have worked to build the good life that we enjoy.

16

Many migrant workers are poor people from Mexico. They know they can earn more money in the United States than they can in the *pueblos* (PWEB-lohs) or small towns in Mexico where they were born. Working as a migrant is often the only kind of job open to people when they move to the United States from Mexico. They come to the United States with very little education or training. Because they can't speak English, they don't always understand the laws of this country. People can easily take advantage of them.

La frontera is 2,000 miles long, and there are lots of small towns with bridges across the Rio Grande where people can enter the United States legally. Immigration officials stop them to review their passports and papers. Near my home in Rio Grande City, there are two towns where people can cross over from Mexico: Roma, just a few miles to the west, and Reynosa, to the east.

There are also large numbers of migrant workers who cross the border illegally, without a passport or entry papers. Instead of using the bridge crossings, they wait for night to come. Then they swim, ride horseback, or cross the Rio Grande in boats. Undocumented persons are sometimes called "wetbacks," because they often get wet coming to the United States.

Most migrants are like my family, legal residents of the United States. My family has permission from the government to live and work here. Legal residents are given "green cards," permits to work in the United States that have been printed on green paper. Many legal residents eventually become citizens. Even when they do, however, their jobs and their way of life make it hard for them to vote. To register to vote, a person must have a permanent address. Many migrants don't have one because they have to move so often.

Some Facts about Children Who Work as Migrants

☐ In the United States, it is against the law for children to work except in agriculture.

☐ Migrant children of any age, with their parents' permission, may work on farms not covered by minimum wage rules. Many farms fall into this category, as they pay workers by how much they pick or pack rather than by the hour.

☐ Minors, sixteen years old or older, are allowed to work with scissors, pruning shears, sharp knives called machetes (mah-SHET-tees), and farm machinery. They can work in places where they might be exposed to dangerous chemicals or pesticides.

☐ Only four out of every ten migrant children attend school beyond the ninth grade.

☐ Only one in ten migrant children finishes high school.

☐ Many migrant children must work rather than attend school. As adults, they can't find better jobs because they lack education.

☐ No one knows how many people work as migrants in the United States. Some experts estimate that there are over a million people who make their living by working in the fields. More than a third of these are women and children under the age of fourteen.

☐ Migrant workers in the United States are not protected by the same federal laws that govern the hours, wages, and union membership for factory workers.

Young Migrant Workers in the Rio Grande Valley

These students live in Rio Grande City, Texas. Although each is only in the fifth or sixth grade, he or she has experienced the life of a migrant worker. They have all decided that they do not want to work in the fields when they grow up.

Luisana

Luisana was born in California.

I started traveling with my family when I was six years old. We drove a long way to Shafter, California. I lived in a place called a labor camp. My mom worked in the fields hoeing cotton, and my dad hauled alfalfa hay in his truck.

I did not work in the harvest. I helped at home by baby-sitting my sister while my parents were working. For fun, we went swimming in the public pool. Now I play sports and hang around with my friends when we go to the labor camp.

I do not want to be a migrant when I grow up. It's hard. It's better for kids to get an education. There are lots of Mexicans who have to work in the fields because they do not know English.

Edith

Edith was born in Texas.

I was eleven years old the first time I went to work in the fields. Traveling there is fun because we play games along the way and listen to the radio. Our parents stop every now and then to buy ice cream cones and potato chips for us to eat.

But when we get to the farms, it's hard because we are not used to the new place. We have to get up early to work and we are tired. There are weeds in the fields that are taller than we are. We have to cut them down. It's very hard work. We get up at five in the morning and work for ten, eleven, and sometimes twelve hours each day.

When I grow up, I want to be a lawyer, teacher, or doctor.

Betty

Betty was born in Mexico.

When we go to work in the summers, we travel to Shafter, California, near Bakersfield. I like it because I have a lot of friends who go there, too. We go to California in a truck that is like a camper. My parents ride in the front. We put blankets in the back and go to sleep. We stop every three hours to eat. I enjoy going because my parents buy me everything I want.

My parents work in the cotton and cut weeds. They pick grapes and pack them in boxes.

I want to be a lawyer when I grow up because all my teachers say I'm good at arguing. I want to help the good people and sue the ones that do them harm.

Laura

Laura was born in Mexico.

I have been working in the fields each summer since I was ten. Usually we go to Minnesota to weed cotton. Our boss is nice. One day, when it was real hot, he gave us all some watermelons to eat.

Working in the fields is kind of boring. It gets really hot. It's humid. This summer we're going to work in the cotton fields of Arkansas.

When I grow up, I want to be a movie star or a singer.

Orlando

Orlando was born in Texas.

I have two brothers and one sister. I am the youngest. I went to work in the fields when I was seven years old. I worked in the grape vineyards in California. We always travel with a few other families. We live in the camps together. It is fun to see my friends there.

My dad has another job in Texas. My mom stays at home to take care of us. Both my parents speak Spanish.

When I grow up, I'd like to be a policeman.

César Chávez

(1927 – 1993)

César Chávez is a hero to many migrant workers. He grew up in Yuma, Arizona, on the small farm that his grandfather had homesteaded in the 1880s. During the hard times of the 1930s, César's family lost the farm. At ten years of age, César was suddenly thrust into the life of a migrant worker, traveling with his family to work in the fields of California's fertile Imperial Valley. This was one of the few opportunities open to his family, people with a lifetime of farming skills but very little formal education.

As a child, César Chávez experienced firsthand the hard conditions of a migrant's life. His family was on the move constantly, looking for work in California's vineyards, fields, and packing sheds. He attended about thirty different schools during his childhood. Then, in 1942, César's father was hurt in a car accident. Although César had not yet entered high school or finished the eighth grade, he had to quit school to help support his family.

The Chávez family picked many kinds of crops. In January, they harvested cabbage, lettuce, and broccoli. In the summer, they picked beans, chili peppers, and corn. In August, they harvested grapes, prunes, cucumbers, and tomatoes. Between October and Christmas, the family worked in the cotton fields.

As César Chávez grew older, he learned about factory workers in the United States who had found ways to change their poor working conditions. These workers formed unions. As a group, they got the owners of the factories to listen to their problems and help them find solutions. They learned that there was power in unity. Slowly, through the efforts of the unions, factory working conditions and wages began to improve.

César Chávez devoted his life to helping migrant farm workers build a union of their own. He wanted to do something for his people, who were among the poorest paid workers in America. He knew their problems because he had suffered along with them.

César Chávez went into the fields to talk to workers. He met them in their homes. He inspired them to participate, offer ideas, and support each other. He encouraged the workers to join the new union for farm workers and to rely on nonviolent methods for achieving change.

In 1965, César Chávez and more than a thousand families of union members went on strike against the grape growers in California. They set up pickets and refused to work in the fields. They called it *La Huelga (lah HWEL-gah)*, which is Spanish for "the strike." They also called for a boycott. As a result, millions of people all across America decided to stop buying grapes to show their sympathy with the farm workers. Together, the strike and the boycott brought attention to the terrible conditions under which the migrants were working. By 1970, many grape growers were willing to work with the new union — the United Farm Workers of America.

In the years since the union was formed, there have been many changes in both wages and working conditions for migrant farm workers. Union members receive higher pay, family health coverage, and even some retirement benefits.

César Chávez died on April 23, 1993. In 1994, César Chávez became the first Mexican-American to receive the Presidential Medal of Freedom, one of the highest honors to be awarded to a citizen of the United States. The award was presented to César's wife, Helen Chávez, by President Bill Clinton.

© Bob Fitch/Black Star

César Chávez holds a flag with the symbol of the United Farm Workers Union, an Aztec eagle. This flag symbolizes the strength and the unity of the farm workers in their struggle for a better life. The flag has a white background if the people are mourning the passing of a loved one. When the workers strike, picket, demonstrate, or attend a parade, the eagle is black against a bright red background.

The United Farm Workers of America,

the union that César Chávez helped to organize, has helped to bring about the following changes for farm workers:

☐ Growers have been encouraged to make the working conditions safer for the farm workers. The growers must wait for several days after pesticides have been sprayed on the fields before allowing workers to enter them.

☐ Many schools in the places where migrant families work have special educational programs for migrant children.

☐ The Head Start Program operates in some communities where migrant workers live. Young children spend their days in a safe environment, enjoying good nutrition, and learning things that will prepare them for entering school.

☐ Laws were passed to insure that growers provide toilets in the fields and cool drinking water.

☐ Farm workers were able to begin getting unemployment insurance for the time they were without work.

☐ In 1973, a new law was passed to provide vocational training for adult migrants.

My School

My parents came to live in the United States to find a better life for my sisters, my brothers, and me. They want us to have a decent education so we can get a good job when we grow up. My mother and father stopped going to school in the third grade because they had to help their parents work in the fields. Now, they think it's very important for us to go to school. That is why my father works in Chicago — to earn money so that my brothers, my sisters, and I can stay in Rio Grande City and attend the same school during the year.

My school is great. I like it because we have a great principal named Chon Garza. He is the son of Mexican parents who came to the United States in the 1940s. He once told me proudly, "My mother and father never felt shame about who they were or where they came from. I never imagined we were poor. I thought everyone lived like us."

Encarnacion "Chon" Garza is the principal of Ringgold Elementary School.

The school that Ricky attends was once a military fort. Ringgold Elementary has about 800 students, nearly half of whom are migrants. The student population is 99.9 percent Hispanic.

Chon Garza takes a personal interest in all of his students. He pays special attention to the needs of migrant children like Ricky.

Mr. Garza's parents first lived in a rough shelter close to Rio Grande City. His father built it out of three pieces of corrugated tin. Soon, however, his family was able to share a house with another family in a labor camp. There was very little privacy, but it was still home. That is where Mr. Garza was born.

Chon Garza's father worked hard. Quickly he earned the respect of the farmers. His mother worked, too, but not in the fields. She cooked and washed clothes for the single men who lived in the camp, and she cared for the children in the family.

Before long, Mr. Garza's father became the foreman on the farm. This meant that Chon's family could live in one place and not travel. His father was really good at his job. He kept it for more than thirty years.

(Top) The principal, Chon Garza, visits the home of a migrant family. The young girl to whom he is speaking attends Ringgold Elementary School. Mr. Garza surprises her when he tells her that, as a boy, he lived in the very same house that she lives in now.

(Left) Today Chon Garza can afford to live in a nice house. He has been successful in his life.

It was not easy going to school when Mr. Garza was a boy. Kids were made to feel bad about their Mexican heritage. They didn't know how to speak English, and Spanish wasn't allowed, so most children did not say anything at all.

I'm lucky because my school isn't like that. At Ringgold Elementary, we have a bilingual program. Kids start studying in Spanish right away and learn to speak English as they go along. Many of our teachers speak Spanish too. We have lots of opportunities to celebrate our heritage. We are proud of who we are.

Mr. Elias Saenz, Ricky's English teacher, works with him on a lesson in reading. Sometimes students who speak Spanish at home have to struggle hard to learn English.

At Ringgold Elementary, Mr. Garza greets the students over the loudspeaker at the beginning of each day. On the blackboard, there is a special Word for the Day. For example, the word "tolerance" is written on the board here. In each classroom, the children discuss the meaning of the word and try to keep it in mind during the school day.

Mr. Garza drops into the classroom whenever he has the chance. He looks in to see what Ricky is working on in the computer lab. He believes that learning to use a computer is important for a student's success in school. Ringgold Elementary has a large computer lab, and students begin to use it in the first grade.

Each year, students at Ringgold Elementary participate in a cultural celebration. They perform Mexican songs and dances in the auditorium for parents and kids from other schools. Mr. Garza, the Master of Ceremonies, is hard to miss in his *huge* sombrero (som-BREH-roh).

Kids gather on the playground for a quick game of marbles. Ricky wins a few shooters before the bus arrives to take the kids home.

(Left) Mr. Garza signs his autograph on a student's shirt. The kids wear red shirts that have the Ringgold Elementary School logo on them for the day they celebrate school spirit. They also wear the shirts when the state of Texas exams are given, because they are proud of their school and themselves.

Hervey Hernandez and Eleazar Garcia must leave school before the year ends. They will go with their families to work in the fields in Illinois and Georgia. Chon Garza calls them to his office to give them a school pin. He also gives each of them a postcard to send to the school once they reach their destination. Mr. Garza feels it is important for these kids to know that someone is thinking about them back "home" and waiting for them to return.

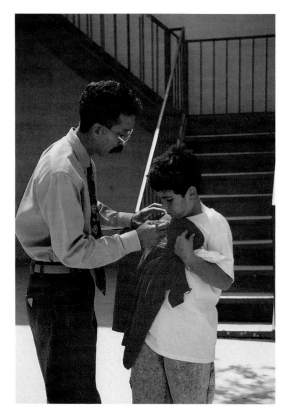

The school year is almost over. Soon my family and many others in Rio Grande City will be packing up their cars, trucks, and campers to begin their migration north. For several months, we will be living in other communities, far from our homes on la frontera.

Migrant workers will pick the grapes in California and the strawberries in Oregon. Some will harvest the peaches in Georgia and the apples in Washington State. Others will pick the broccoli in New Jersey and the lettuce in Florida. Many of the fresh fruits and vegetables that end up on the tables of Americans will be there because of our labor.

Across the street from Ricky's house, his mother attends a neighborhood meeting with Mr. Garza and other parents and teachers from the school. They come together to discuss the problems their students are having and to find solutions. In this colonia, parents care a great deal about the education of their children and take an active role in shaping their futures.

Ricky and his schoolmates join Chon Garza and their vice-principal, Amador Lupe, Jr., in a school cheer.

I am proud to be able to work with my family. I am happy to be able to help my parents, but I am also glad that they have chosen to give me a chance for a better future. It is good to be a student at Ringgold Elementary and I am lucky to graduate to the sixth grade. Not everyone in my class has that opportunity.

My friend, Chon Garza, has taught me that the best way to make my dreams come true is to get a good education. With an education, anything is possible.

GLOSSARY

bilingual: When a person is able to speak his or her own language and another one equally well.

boycott: When people refuse to buy a product as a form of protest.

César Chávez: *(SAY-sahr CHAH-vez)* (1927 - 1993) A Mexican-American migrant worker who helped to establish the United Farm Workers of America, the first successful labor union for agricultural workers in the United States.

chamberlains: (CHAM-ber-lehns) The male escorts at the *quinceañera* celebration.

colonias: *(coh-LONE-ee-ahs)* A Spanish term for housing developments in the United States that run along the border. They are also found near the border in Mexico.

damas: (DAH-mahs) The female escorts at the *quinceañera* celebration.

la frontera: *(lah fron-TEHR-rah)* The Spanish term for the area in the United States just north of the Mexican border.

green card: A slang term for a permit that allows foreigners to work in the United States. It gets its nickname from the green paper on which the permit is printed.

la huelga: (lah HWEL-gah) The Spanish words for "the strike."

immigrant: A person who moves from one country to live in another.

labor camps: A group of small houses or apartments in or near farms where migrant people can live temporarily while they are working.

machete: *(mah-SHET-tee)* The Spanish term for a long, sharp knife used to cut through tough grasses or brush.

macho: *(MAH-cho)* A Spanish term that means "manly" or "masculine."

manual labor: A type of work that is done by hand.

migrant worker: A worker who moves from place to place to work in agricultural jobs.

migration: The process of moving from one place to another.

Miguel Alemán: *(mee-GEL ah-lay-MON)* A small town in Mexico, near Rio Grande City, Texas.

pesticides: Chemicals that poison insects that attack crops.

pueblo: *(PWEB-loh)* The Spanish term for "town."

quinceañera: *(KEEN-say-ahn-NEYR-rah)* The Spanish term for a special party given by parents when their daughter reaches fifteen years of age.

raspas: *(RAHS-pahs)* The Spanish term for "snow cones."

Rio Grande Valley: A large, fertile valley along the Rio Grande River.

sandia: *(san-DEE-AH)* The Spanish term for "watermelon."

sombrero: *(som-BREH-roh)* The Spanish term for a hat with a large brim.

sorghum: *(SAWR-guhm)* A crop grown in the Rio Grande Valley of Texas that is used as feed for animals.

strike: When employees agree to refuse to work for a period of time as a protest against the employer, usually for higher wages or better working conditions.

tejano music: *(teh-HAHN-noh)* A type of music popular in Mexico and along the border in the United States that combines songs with instruments like guitars and accordions.

undocumented person: An individual who enters the United States without the government's permission.

union: An organization of workers with the authority to bargain with the employer for better wages and working conditions for its members.

wetbacks: Slang term for undocumented persons from Mexico.

INDEX

RIO GRANDE CITY, TEXAS

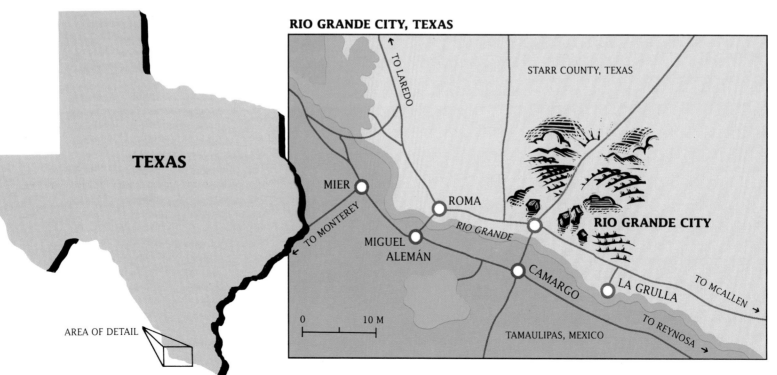